To ....

From ....

Date ....

Gettin' Old Ain't for WiMpS!

KAREN O'CONNOR

HARVEST HOUSE PUBLISHERS

EUGENE, OREGON

Gettin' Old Ain't for Wimps Gift Edition

Text copyright © 2004 by Karen O'Connor

Photography copyright © 2012 M.I.L.K. Licensing Limited. All rights reserved.
www.milkphotos.com

Published by Harvest House Publishers
Eugene, Oregon 97402
www.harvesthousepublishers.com

ISBN 978-0-7369-2600-3

Published in association with the literary agency of Janet Kobobel Grant, Books & Such, 4788 Carissa Avenue, Santa Rosa, California 95405

Design and production by Dugan Design Group, Bloomington, Minnesota

Select text is adapted from *Gettin' Old Ain't for Wimps* by Karen O'Connor, Copyright © 2004

All Scripture quotations are taken from The Holy Bible, *New International Version® NIV®*. Copyright © 1973, 1978, 1984, 2011 by Biblica, Inc.™ Used by permission. All rights reserved worldwide.

Printed in China

15 16 17 18 19 20 / FC / 10 9 8 7 6 5 4 3 2

For all the women in my life.
May we age with hope, humility, and humor.

Even to your old age and gray hairs
I am he, I am he who will sustain you.
I have made you and I will carry you;
I will sustain you and I will rescue you.
—Isaiah 46:4

Contents

Something to Look Forward To

My husband and I were browsing in a gift shop during a visit to Lexington, Kentucky. A plaque on the wall caught my eye:

Don't complain about growing old…
Few people get the privilege!

We smiled at the wisdom of those few words. How blessed we felt in that moment—to realize we had successfully reached our sixth and seventh decades and were still kicking and laughing. I suddenly got excited about all the possibilities still ahead—adventures, risks, funny experiences, the "stuff" of life that keeps us young at heart regardless of the circumstances.

That "stuff" is the heart of this book. I hope you'll enjoy the humorous stories and inspirations included here, each one tied to a real-life incident, so that by the time you finish reading, you'll agree that getting old ain't for wimps! It's for people like you and me, who want to keep on loving, living, and laughing all the way home to heaven.

KAREN O'CONNOR
Watsonville, California

Say It Again, Sam!

> The most thoroughly wasted of all days is that on which one has not laughed.
>
> Nicolas Chamfort

Carl, aged 81, had his eye on Darlene, aged 79. The two had met at a dance for seniors one week and had been seeing each other ever since—rather, *trying* to see each other.

Both were a bit hard-of-hearing, but that was okay. They could sympathize with one another over their mutual lack. Carl invited Darlene to lunch one afternoon in the city. "Meet you at Fifth and Forty-ninth at one o'clock," he shouted into the telephone.

"Fine by me," said Darlene. "I'll take the early afternoon bus and see you then."

The following day Darlene boarded the bus at the corner near her apartment house and enjoyed the ride, excited about her date with the handsome Carl. She even allowed her mind to wander into the future. Maybe they'd be married someday—soon—she hoped since at their ages, time was truly running out.

8

Darlene stepped down from the bus when it arrived at her destination. No Carl. She waited and waited. Then she took out the paper she'd used to scribble the time and place. Sure enough. She got it right. By one thirty she began to worry that something terrible had happened to Carl. By one forty-five she was in a huff. She'd been stood up! *The nerve of him*, she thought. *It's not as though he is a young buck with women lined up down the block just to spend an afternoon with him.*

Darlene caught the next bus home. As she walked in the door, the phone rang. It was Carl. She didn't know whether to listen to him or hang up.

"Where were you?" he asked. "I waited and waited."

"Where were *you*?" Darlene shouted. "*I* waited."

"I was there—right where I said I'd be," said Carl. "Fifth and Forty-ninth at one o'clock."

Darlene felt her face grow warm with embarrassment. "I was at *Sixth* and Forty-ninth at one o'clock," she replied, "just as I thought you said."

They both laughed and set a new date—to shop for hearing aids!

REFLECTION

*Like an earring of gold or an ornament
of fine gold is the rebuke of a wise judge to a listening ear.*

Proverbs 25:12

JUST BETWEEN GOD AND ME

*Lord, I need a rebuke now and again. I think I know what I'm doing. I think I hear what I
need to get. I think I'm on target, only to find out I missed by a wide margin. Whew! What
a lesson in humility. Keep me on track, O Lord, and do not let my pride get in the way of
hearing and doing your Word.*

The Honeymooners

My husband stood in the lobby of the Wyndham Hotel in San Diego, California, ready for a day's work—ushering convention-goers into the correct limo or bus to be chauffeured to the airport. As men and women poured out of the elevators, he held up a sign with their company's name on it, and motioned the crowd in the direction they should go.

At one point an elderly couple emerged and walked slowly toward the front door. Charles rushed over to assist them. "Are you with my group?" he asked, holding up his sign so they could read it easily.

"No, no," said the man. "We're on our honeymoon."

That response sparked Charles's interest. "Your honeymoon? How wonderful. Congratulations!" he said, smiling broadly. "Where are you going?"

"We're visiting our four grown children," said the man. "She has two, and I have two."

To love is to find pleasure in the happiness of the person loved.

Gottfried Willhelm Leibniz

If I had a rose for every time I thought of you,
I'd be picking roses for a lifetime.

Swedish Proverb

Yes, we must
ever be friends;
and of all
who offer
you friendship,
let me be
the first,
the truest,
the nearest
and dearest!

Henry Wadsworth
Longfellow

"How nice of you to spend your honeymoon with your kids," said Charles. "I hope they appreciate it."

"They certainly do," said the gentleman. "You see our trip got a bit delayed. We were married last January, and here it is November and we're just now ready to go. My wife, here," he added, touching her arm fondly, "got so excited about our marriage that she broke her hip the day after the wedding! We've had to stay put ever since," he added and laughed out loud.

Charles joined him. It was pretty funny in a weird sort of way. The man and woman bantered back and forth as Charles took in every word. The woman playfully accused her husband of exaggerating, and then reminded him that on their wedding night he had misplaced his hearing aid, and they spent half the night looking for it. "Now you tell me," she said, looking at Charles, "who you think was the most excited."

"I'm not going to touch that one," said Charles, backing away playfully.

"Tell me, how did you meet?" my husband asked, eager for more details.

"In an assisted living facility," she said. "We were sitting at the same dinner table one night."

"How nice that you found one another!" Charles added.

"I'm sure happy," said the man, "though I'm not sure what's in store for

me. You see," he said, cupping his hands around his mouth as if to guard a secret, "I married an older woman."

His wife poked him in the ribs with her elbow, but that didn't stop him.

"She's 84," he said, for all to hear, "and I'm only 81!"

He redeemed himself fast before she bopped him over the head with her handbag.

"We might be in our eighties," he said whimsically, "but we're the two luckiest kids on the block."

Charles had to agree.

13

REFLECTION

*For this reason a man will leave his father and mother and be united to his wife,
and the two will become one flesh.*

Ephesians 5:31

JUST BETWEEN GOD AND ME

*Dear Lord, what a charming story. I love knowing that people can still find a loving
relationship even when time seems to be running out. You bring men and women
together in marriage to comfort and please, to help and to enjoy one another. Thank you,
God, that you care about your people, and you give each one what is right
according to your perfect will.*

Are we not like two volumes of one book?

Marceline Desbordes-Valmore

My, How You've Changed!

Mary Beth observed her sister-in-law showing pictures of herself when she was young to her granddaughter, Audrey. The two enjoyed leafing through the album that displayed Grandma from birth to adulthood.

As they closed the album, Audrey's grandma looked at her to see what comment, if any, she had about seeing her as a child and teen. It's hard for little kids to imagine that adults were ever children themselves.

Audrey looked up and turned to her grandmother with a quizzical expression. "Grandma, whatever happened to your face?"

Laughter is the sun that drives winter
from the human face.

Victor Hugo

REFLECTION

*Charm is deceptive, and beauty is fleeting; but a woman who fears the L*ORD *is to be praised.*

Proverbs 31:30

JUST BETWEEN GOD AND ME

Lord, I'm aware of how quickly my face is changing. I thought it would be years and years before I looked like my grandparents, but here I am—an older person myself—with wrinkles and loose skin of my own. It seems only yesterday that it was firm and smooth. I'm so relieved to know that you have your eye on the part of me that really matters—the condition and appearance of my soul.

Chicken-Feet Hands

When Freda's two daughters, Janet and Julie, were young, Freda had a custom of inviting two elderly sisters to lunch each year. The ladies lived out of state, so their annual get-together was a special treat for everyone. "The elder was a 'spinster,'" said Freda, "and the younger, a grandmother."

On one of their visits, Freda's daughters were quite excited about having company for lunch. They invited the elderly sisters to join them in play, such as ring-around-the-rosy.

The elder sister, the more outgoing of the two, joined right in. Julie, Freda's younger daughter, even invited her to ride her bike—surely a sign of how welcome they were. Much to Freda's relief, the woman declined!

As they held hands during a game, Julie stared at Aunt Sally's hands. Then she blurted out, "Aunt Sally, why do your hands look like chicken feet?"

Let us be grateful to people who make us happy; they are the charming gardeners who make our souls blossom.

Marcel Proust

"I thought I would die of embarrassment," said Freda. "I reprimanded my very confused child, who had no idea she had insulted her elderly playmate."

Thankfully, Aunt Sally came to Freda's rescue. She laughed with genuine amusement. "Why, they do look like chicken feet!" she said and kept right on playing.

"Now, *I'm* a senior," said Freda. "And the tables have been turned. Recently, while teaching the four- and five-year-olds in Sunday school, a new four-year-old girl named Hannah joined us."

"Why are you both so old?" the child asked Freda's co-teacher, who is about the same age as Freda. The woman tried to explain the aging process in terms a four-year-old could understand—not an easy thing to do.

Freda said she is now preparing for other unexpected and intrusive questions. Maybe one of them will be, "Miss Freda, why do your hands look like chicken feet?"

That day is lost on which one has not laughed.

French Proverb

REFLECTION

He lifted me out of the slimy pit, out of the mud and mire; he set my feet on a rock and gave me a firm place to stand.

Psalm 40:2

JUST BETWEEN GOD AND ME

Lord, kids can really blow us away with their frank questions and surprising observations. At first I feel insulted, but then I think maybe that's just what I need at this stage of life— a good honest look at myself, chicken-feet hands and all. As long as you have given me a firm place to stand—on your love and on your Word—then what does it matter how my hands look?

21

Seeing Is Believing

Friendship!
The precious gold
of life.
By age refined,
yet ever new.
Tried in the
crucible of time
it always rings
true.

Joseph Shaylor

One day I had a near-panic attack when I couldn't find my glasses," said Bea. "I only use them for reading, but that day I really did need them."

Bea's friend and neighbor was visiting, so they both looked high and low, under and on top of all surfaces, but neither of them could come up with the missing glasses.

"I emptied my purse," said Bea, "checked my pockets, looked again in every conceivable place, to no avail."

Finally she decided, "Forget it. They'll turn up eventually. We were about to leave the house when I looked in the bathroom mirror, and there they were—perched on top of my head! I didn't realize it till that moment and, funnier still, my neighbor didn't see them there either! We laughed until we cried."

I doubt Bea or her neighbor will ever choose one another as a partner in a treasure hunt!

REFLECTION

Moreover, our eyes failed, looking in vain for help.

Lamentations 4:17

JUST BETWEEN GOD AND ME

Lord, you know the saying "two heads are better than one." It's not foolproof, though. Sometimes two people are in the same mind-set, and they can't free themselves up, so they both get lost looking for what is right under their noses or perched on top of their heads. How well I know this from experience. But when I call on your Holy Spirit for help, he's right there leading, guiding, and practically pointing to the very thing I need— whether it's my glasses or a new way of looking at things. Thank you for your Spirit, O Lord.

True happiness renders men kind and sensible; and that happiness
is always shared with others.

Charles de Secondat

Smoke Screen

Now that Max and I no longer have to show our ID cards in order to qualify for the senior menu at IHOP or a senior discount at the movies," said Diana, "we've developed a sense of humor about the benefits and perils of growing older."

One year, a few weeks before Christmas, four of their grandchildren were spending the day with Diana and Max. The kids were helping their grandmother wrap gifts. One of the presents was a smoke alarm for their father, Diana's son.

"I asked if they had a smoke alarm in their house," said Diana. "They thought there was one, but no one seemed to know if it was still in good working order. I mentioned that ours wasn't working either."

Max overheard this brief conversation and decided to check theirs. "I'll have a look and test it," he said as he headed down the hall toward the spot where they had initially installed the alarm.

As gold more
splendid from
the fire appears;
Thus friendship
brightens by the
length of years.

Thomas Carlyle

An effort made for the happiness of
others lifts above ourselves.

Lydia Child

"The kids and I heard Max striking several matches," said Diana, "but nothing followed. A loud screech would have signaled that the alarm was working."

"Probably needs a new battery," Max hollered.

"What size does it take?" Diana called from the living room.

"That's funny," Max replied. "There's no place for a battery in this thing."

Diana could sense the frustration in his voice.

She and the kids walked down the hallway to see what was going on. Suddenly Max chuckled. Then they all burst into laughter as they realized Max had been holding the lighted matches under the ringer box for their electric doorbell.

"The smoke alarm was about five feet farther down the hall," said Diana. "He tested it, and it worked just fine."

Friendship! The beauteous soul of life
Which gladdens youth and strengthens age;
May it our hearts and lives entwine
Together on life's fleeting page.

Joseph Shaylor

REFLECTION

Teach me knowledge and good judgment, for I trust your commands.

Psalm 119:66

JUST BETWEEN GOD AND ME

I can't help but laugh, O Lord, when I make silly mistakes, especially when on second glance the right thing to do was so obvious. But sometimes my actions also scare me, especially as I'm growing older. I wonder if I'm beginning to lose it—or if I already have! Your Word saves me from these worries. You continually promise that you will give me the knowledge I need to make wise judgments. Thank you for that assurance.

Palm Reader

Judy and I became friends over the phone. I called her regarding some information I needed for one of my writing projects, and we were practically "buds" by the time we hung up. I remember wishing we lived closer so we could get together for a walk or tea or dinner with our husbands.

Laugh, if thou art wise.

Marcus Aurelius

Once, after we hung up, I shot Judy an e-mail, thanking her for her time. She wrote back inviting my husband and me to visit if we ever came to Seattle. "Keep our phone number and address in your PalmPilot," she said.

Oh no! I thought. *She assumes I have state-of-the-art technology—and I don't.* I was embarrassed to admit that I not only don't own a PalmPilot, I'm not even sure what you do with one. I like the tried-and-true paper calendar.

> We are shaped and fashioned by what we love.
>
> Johann Wolfgang von Goethe

I stewed for a moment or two and then decided to make light of it. "I don't have a PalmPilot," I replied by e-mail. "But I have two palms. Does it count if I scribble your name and address on one of them? And make a copy on the other?"

REFLECTION

I thank my God every time I remember you.

Philippians 1:3

JUST BETWEEN GOD AND ME

I am blessed with good friends, dear God. Thank you for them—those of many years and those new in my life. I want to keep in touch with them all, but that's impossible. You can help me, Lord, to remember them in prayer, at least. And if I can't recall every name, I can rest in the certainty that you know their names. By your Spirit not one will slip out from under your careful watch.

33

Time to Move

Edith decided in her early eighties that it was time to sell her family home and move to smaller quarters. Roger, from the Seniors Ministry at her church, offered to help organize her possessions and pack up what she planned to take with her. As the two moved toward a collection of books, Roger picked up a volume and leafed through it.

"There's a funny story behind that book," said Edith whimsically. "When my husband, Hubert, was still alive, he filled our basement with books," she added, rolling her eyes at just the thought of the overwhelming personal library he had amassed without her agreement.

"Years ago one of our neighbors was planning a fund-raiser garage sale. She was collecting old books from everyone on the block. I quickly packed up three boxes of our books and gave them to her, but I never told Hubert," Edith said, chuckling.

The morning of the sale, Edith and Hubert paid a visit to their

A laugh, to be joyous, must flow from a joyous heart, for without kindness, there can be no true joy.

Thomas Carlyle

On with the dance! Let joy be unconfined!

Lord Byron

neighbor's garage to support her effort to raise charitable funds. As they walked through the rows of books, Edith suddenly heard Hubert shout from across the room.

"Oh, Momma," he called, raising a particular book in his hand.

"Look!" proclaimed Hubert. "It's that book I've been wanting for so long!"

Edith couldn't help but laugh all over again. "Roger, it was the very book you're holding now," she said. "One from Hubert's own collection. He snatched up the copy and walked right over to the cashier and plunked down his money—paying for the book a second time. I never did tell him that he bought back his own book," said Edith. "And I'm not sure to this day he ever read it."

REFLECTION

For in him we live and move and have our being.

Acts 17:28

JUST BETWEEN GOD AND ME

Moving can be a good thing—though it's hard to give up the familiar. But I think it's important to stay in reality, especially as I get older. I don't need as much space as I used to. And I can get along with fewer possessions. I thank you, Lord, for the large home we had when our family needed it. But now I can be content wherever I live as long as you are with me and I am with you.

Changes

Carol admits that growing old is not so bad—especially when you consider the alternative. She likes to remember the old saying, "Age is mostly a matter of mind. If you don't mind, it doesn't matter."

Some of the changes in the world around her, however, do bother her. "For example," she asks, "why have the clothing manufacturers changed their sizing scale? What used to be a size 12 dress is now a size 16. Didn't they think we would notice these things? I'm also convinced that people who make bathroom scales have also changed their dials. There's no way I'd ever let myself weigh as much as my scale registers!"

Carol has also observed that department store clerks have started whispering. "I don't know why this sudden change," she says, bewildered. She could hear them just fine ten years ago!

Getting old ain't for wimps—it's true. In fact, getting older, period,

We don't
laugh
because we're
happy—
we're happy
because
we laugh.

William James

The greatest happiness of life is the conviction that we are loved, loved for ourselves, or rather loved in spite of ourselves.

Victor Hugo

> A good laugh
> is sunshine
> in the house.
>
> William Makepeace
> Thackeray

is not really the problem. It's all the other stuff going on around us. "Have you gone up a flight of stairs recently?" asks Carol. "They're making them a lot steeper than they used to. I can remember when going up a flight of stairs was nothing. Now they're so steep I have to stop halfway to catch my breath."

Carol has a few comments, as well, about how fast people drive these days. She and her daughter were out one day together, and it was so dangerous even her daughter had white knuckles. "She cautioned me," said Carol, "to look in the rearview mirror before I pulled onto the highway.

"I reminded her of my impeccable driving record," said Carol. "But the next time I was out I did look in the mirror, and all I have to say is, it's a good thing cars have brakes. The way *other* people screeched and swerved around me, it's no wonder there are so many accidents these days."

Growing older does require some preparation. "It's the responsible thing to do," claims Carol. She and her husband put their financial affairs in order and drew up a family trust.

"I thought everything went well, until we were finishing up and our oldest daughter turned to her dad and said, 'Daddy, please don't die first and leave her for us to take care of.'

"The older I get, the one thing that bothers me the most," said Carol, "is that my friends in heaven will think I didn't make it."

REFLECTION

He changes times and seasons; he deposes kings and raises up others. He gives wisdom to the wise and knowledge to the discerning.

Daniel 2:21

JUST BETWEEN GOD AND ME

Lord, thanks so much for being on my team even when my fellow "teammates" shake their heads and chuckle at my behavior. Sometimes I get exasperated with myself too. I'd like to be able to sail up the stairs as I used to, see a lower number on the scale when I weigh myself, drive and talk at the same time without risking the safety of those with me, but I can't do what I once did. Times are a-changing, and I must go with the flow of getting older. I pray for continued wisdom and discernment now and in the days and years ahead.

New Every Morning

Lonnie could hardly wait to show her husband the walking path she'd discovered not far from home. Lined with trees and songbirds, it ran between two lakes. The beauty and solitude provided a pleasant escape from the noise and busyness of suburbia.

One day they stole away for a walk. This was Lonnie's opportunity to take Ray to her new spot. When they arrived, Ray looked around. He didn't appear impressed with the beauty or uniqueness of the setting.

"We've been here before," he said.

Lonnie was disappointed. That wasn't the reaction she'd hoped for.

"No, we haven't," she protested.

"Yes, we have," he insisted. "We biked here a couple of years ago."

Lonnie strained to remember. Finally she laughed it off.

Breathless, we flung us on a windy hill, laughed in the sun, and kissed the lovely grass.

Rupert Brooke

43

"Well, there's one advantage to forgetfulness," she said with a smile. "Every day is fresh, and every experience is new. God does cause all things to work together for good, doesn't he?"

Lonnie and Ray linked hands and went for a walk on their "new" path.

REFLECTION

You make known to me the path of life; you will fill me with joy in your presence, with eternal pleasures at your right hand.

Psalm 16:11

JUST BETWEEN GOD AND ME

Lord, when I get up with the birds, pull on my duds, and pound my way around the block or through the park, I feel energized. It's a great way to start my day! Why don't I make a habit of it then? I give in to small excuses. I'm tired. I have urgent business. I had a bad night. It's cloudy and gray. Help me, Lord, to overcome my reasons and to focus instead on the benefit—the joy of your presence under the sky and sun you created for me.

Heartthrob

Celebrate love.
It is the breath
of your existence
and the best
of all reasons
for living.

Author Unknown

My sweet mother died in October 2003, at the age of 89. Shortly after she passed on, my sister June handed over some of Mom's diary entries in a book I had given her as a gift on Mother's Day some years before.

I always knew Mom loved our father, and he loved her with equal passion. Everyone who saw them together was aware of their special relationship. Mom was also known for her dry wit and ready humor on all occasions. So I was not surprised to see the two combined in one of her writings in 1992 dedicated to her husband, Phil, my father.

To Phil:

To hit my target heart rate, I can exercise vigorously for twenty minutes—or—I can sit around and think of you.

What greater thing is there for two human souls than to feel that they are joined—to strengthen each other—to be at one with each other in silent unspeakable memories.

George Eliot

REFLECTION

*May the Lord make your love increase and overflow for each other
and for everyone else.*

1 Thessalonians 3:12

JUST BETWEEN GOD AND ME

Lord, you are my heartthrob, my ever-present companion, my first love. Help me to give to others—my family, friends, even strangers—out of the abundance of your love for me. It is good to have the love of a spouse, but it's even better to have the love of the God of the universe.

6004

The photographer's son, Oliver, and his grandma express their affection for each other.
© Jonathan Jones

6095

This couple in Geleen, Netherlands, has been married for sixty years. The building in which they live (seen in the background) was the school which the husband attended as a child, and they are standing in what was once the school playground. © Edith Eussen

6079

Richard and Betty share a tender moment at the wedding of their grandson, Roger, in Dana Point, California, USA.
© Wen-Tzu Chang

6060d

Seniors at a Christmas party held just outside London, UK, celebrate in the traditional way.
© Charlotte Wigg

6057

Jean and Ron from the Gold Coast, Australia, who met as teenagers and were then separated by war, show affection on their sixty-fifth wedding anniversary.
© Wayne Jones

6060c

Seniors at a Christmas party held just outside London, UK, celebrate in the traditional way.
© Charlotte Wigg

6132

Wearing remarkably similar expressions, Evelyn and her great-grandson, Micah, meet for the first and last time at Evelyn's nursing home in Chillicothe, Ohio, USA.
© Stacy Wasmuth

6053

Guests, Ivy, Sarah and baby Harry, are captured at a wedding in Wiltshire, UK.
© Paul O'Connor

6126

Daniel, an artist, and his wife, Vera, pose in their bedroom in their flat in Krivoy Rog, Ukraine. The walls are covered with pictures that have been cut out by Daniel.
© David Graham

6128

A mobile phone connects a faraway son with his family in Siliguri, North Bengal, India.
© Bijoy Chowdhury

6055

Identically dressed Shirley and Virginia pose for their portrait at their home in Santa Monica, California, USA.
© Mark Hanauer

6028

In Littleton, Colorado, USA, Sophia gazes up at her Grandpa Tracy.
© Cheryl Jacobs Nicolai

6024

The photographer's son, Lim-Kenji, clips his grandmother's fingernails.
© Sam Lim

3086

Two of a kind, the photographer's great-aunts at their home in Canada. Sisters Rose and Florence have lived together since they were both widowed in their 40s.
© Andrew Danson Danushevsky

6115

A chess game ends in laughter and good cheer in a street in Brussels, Belgium.
© Horia Tudor

6078

Three lifelong friends enjoy Sunday afternoon on a stoop in Buenos Aires, Argentina.
© Todd Winters

6127b

Felicidad and her friend are members of the Kallawaya community in Curva, Bolivia, which is known for its holistic medicine. They have just celebrated a spiritual ceremony and are wearing traditional clothing.
© Jean François Leblanc

3021

The 60th wedding anniversary – love, respect, and six decades of marriage bind husband and wife Henri and Violet Mayoux. They exchange a humorous look as they prepare to cut their anniversary cake in Ontario, Canada.
© Ricardo Ordóñez

6129

Bridegroom Vince shares a pre-wedding moment with his father, Giuseppe, at the family home in Auburn, Sydney, Australia.
© Graham Monro

6084

An elderly man in Narva, Estonia, visits his wife in hospital via the window while other patients look out to the street.
© Andrej Balco

6068

Two friends from the Ifugao province in the Philippines view a mobile phone.
© Raniel Jose Madrazo Castañeda

6034

Two friends catch up on the local gossip at home in northeast Turkey.
© Bob Moore

6113

At Century Village, Florida, USA, friends Pauline and May have just come out of the pool after their water-aerobics class.
© Brian Smith

6060a

Seniors at a Christmas party held just outside London, UK, celebrate in the traditional way.
© Charlotte Wiig

2085

Coney Island in New York, USA, six friends turn a sandy beach into a dance floor to the delight of their enthusiastic audience.
© Yorghos Kontaxis

6003

Long-time friends relax in a bar on Auburn Avenue in downtown Atlanta, Georgia, USA.
© Alicia Hansen

6045

A small boy and his grandfather play basketball in a park in Milan, Italy.
© Silvia Morara

6127a

Prohibited during Mao's political regime, the tango is now popular in China and a couple is free to practise the dance in a Beijing park.
© Jean-François Leblanc

6099

In Ireland, on an afternoon in spring, Mary and Lorna share a cup of tea and a laugh.
© Lorna Fitzsimons

6000

Clara was a friend of the famous suffragettes, the Pankhursts. She lived alone at her home in Essex, UK, into her nineties, with her cat for company.
© Andy Palmer

6060b

Seniors at a Christmas party held just outside London, UK, celebrate in the traditional way.
© Charlotte Wiig

6021

Kyria, an elderly villager from Messinia, Greece, laughs in front of the camera.
© Martina Gemmola

6010

A couple in Kroptewitz, Germany, paint both sides of a fence at the same time.
© Martin Langer

6058

In Warsaw, Poland, the photographer's goddaughter, Hania, embraces her great-grandmother, Maria, whose portrait hangs behind them.
© Katarzyna Mala

1027

Rebecca, aged 20 months, and her grandmother share the simple pleasures of a street festival in Brisbane, Australia.
© Lyn Dowling

2076

An inseparable pair, elderly Ukrainian sisters caught on film during a visit to Cleveland, Ohio, USA.
© Bernard Mendoza

6016a

On her wedding day, the bride, Jessica, hugs her mother whose own wedding portrait hangs above the mantelpiece in her home in North Stonington, Connecticut, USA.
© Melissa Mermin

6040

A couple share an amusing moment in Alexandra Township, near Johannesburg, South Africa.
© Michael Meyersfeld

6054

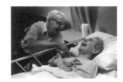

This married couple met in a nursing home. The wife, who is paralysed, shares a joke with her husband.
© Abraham Menashe